THE LIBRARY OF
nutrition™

The Food Pyramid and Basic Nutrition
Assembling the Building Blocks of a Healthy Diet

Graham Faiella

rosen
central™

The Rosen Publishing Group, Inc., New York

For Lynn, my nutrition muse

Published in 2005 by The Rosen Publishing Company, Inc.
29 East 21st Street, New York, NY 10010

First Edition

Library of Congress Cataloging-in-Publication Data

Faiella, Graham.
The food pyramid and basic nutrition : assembling the building blocks of a healthy diet / by Graham Faiella.
   p. cm. — (The library of nutrition)
Includes bibliographical references and index.
ISBN 1-4042-0304-4 (library binding)
1. Nutrition—Juvenile literature. 2. Food—Juvenile literature.
I. Title. II. Series.
TX355.F35 2004
613.2—dc22

2004015969

Manufactured in the United States of America

contents

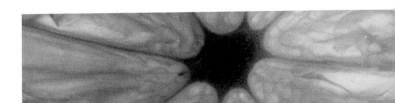

introduction

You are what you eat. This may be a cliché, but it also happens to be true. What goes into your body determines your physical and emotional health. It affects how you feel physically and how you feel about yourself. Food contains the nutrients and energy your body needs to stay alive. The quality of your life—your health and vitality—depends on the balance of foods you eat every day. Understanding what good nutrition is can help you make better choices about your diet and improve your health.

In 1992, the United States Department of Agriculture (USDA) created its now famous food guide pyramid—a simple graphic that outlines the ideal daily balance of different kinds of foods and nutrients that will result in good nutrition and a healthy weight. Since the food guide pyramid was introduced, however, the number of overweight and obese Americans has continued to increase. Results of the 1999–2000 National Health and Nutrition Examination Survey (NHANES) report that an estimated 64 percent of U.S. adults are either overweight or obese. As a result, certain kinds of life-threatening, weight-related diseases and chronic illnesses, such as diabetes, cancer, and heart disease, have increased among Americans.

Given this epidemic of obesity and related increase in disease, is the food pyramid truly a good guide to a better diet? Critics say the guide is too general and too vague, and contains misleading information about the actual nutritional value of some kinds of food that appear on it. They also charge that by leaving out any recommendations for regular physical exercise, the food pyramid misses a vitally important part of the equation for good health.

Whether or not these critics are correct, it would seem that many Americans are either ignoring the recommendations of the food pyramid, selectively applying them, or misinterpreting them. The pyramid is just a guide to good nutrition. It can make recommendations, but it cannot force people to follow them. How you use the nutrition information provided by the food pyramid is up to you.

When following the food pyramid's guidelines, you do not have to carry a calculator around with you to count every single calorie. You do not need to keep in your pocket lists of ingredients and nutrients to analyze everything you

An Indianapolis teenager chooses among healthy food options at his high school cafeteria.

Planning meals, shopping, and cooking together can be a great way for you and your family to learn more about good nutrition together and to support each other in developing eating habits that will lead to longer and healthier lives.

eat. You just need to know a few things about nutrition—what is good for you and what is not so good—to help you make smart decisions about what to eat and what not to eat. You will quickly get into the habit of thinking about what you choose to eat and choosing foods that will help you stay healthy. Before long, proper daily nutrition will be second nature to you.

Before discussing the food pyramid, its components, and its recommendations, it will be useful to review the basic elements of nutrition, some key terms, and the major nutrients.

chapter 1

The Basic Elements of Nutrition

The term "nutrition" refers to all the processes related to the eating and digesting of food and the breaking down of food and its nutrients into energy. It also refers to the processes related to the growth, repair, and maintenance of the living cells of the human body, processes that are fueled by the energy and nutrients provided by the food we eat. In poor countries, millions of people suffer from malnutrition. They do not have enough food to eat, and the food they eat is often of poor quality. Surprisingly, in rich countries like the United States, malnutrition is also a problem. Millions of people eat too much food that is not nutritious, which makes them overweight or obese.

Putting into practice the basic principles of nutrition can help you create a healthy diet, reach and maintain a healthy weight, and enjoy a long and healthy life.

Energy and Calories

Your body is a complex machine that is working all the time, around the clock. At every moment of the day, your heart is

A young girl and her mother walk side by side in Des Plaines, Illinois. According to a 2004 FDA report, 13 percent of children ages six to eleven are obese, double the number of two decades ago. More than 20 percent of U.S. adults are also obese.

beating. Your lungs are taking in air. Blood is circulating through your veins and arteries (the tubelike vessels that carry blood to and from your heart throughout the body). Your bones, muscles, and skin are growing, repairing bits of themselves, and generally keeping themselves in good condition.

Even when you are not doing anything active (when you are sleeping, for example, or lying on the couch and watching television), your body's machinery is working ceaselessly on the inside. This constant work requires energy even if you are lying down or sitting still. You are not always at rest, however. Throughout the day you use your body to perform physical activities. You stand up. You walk and run. You sit down. You eat. You play. This, too, requires energy. Your body gets the energy it needs to function properly from food.

The amount of energy contained in food and the amount of energy your body burns is measured in calories. A calorie is a unit of measure that indicates how much energy a specific food will provide. When we say a particular food has a certain number of calories, what we mean is that the food will provide a certain amount of energy. And when we say a particular activity (like running for thirty minutes) burns a certain number of calories, what we mean is that the activity requires a certain amount of energy.

Calories are a measure of quantity. They measure how much energy is found in the food you eat, as well as how much energy your body uses to keep running smoothly and performing physical and mental activities. According to the Food and Drug Administration (FDA), the typical American needs about 2,000 calories a day, but caloric requirements vary from one person to another. Most people need an amount somewhere between 1,600 and 2,800 calories. Men generally require more calories than women do. Because they are growing—a process that requires larger amounts of energy—children and teenagers require more calories than adults. Most people need fewer calories per day as they get older. Men and women with active lifestyles need more calories than sedentary (nonactive) people who do not burn as much energy through exercise or an otherwise busy daily routine.

Just as important as the quantity of energy we get from food, however, is the quality of that energy. We measure the quality of the energy our food provides by taking into account something else provided by that food—nutrients.

Nutrients

To a greater degree than at any other time in human history, twenty-first-century North Americans have access to an almost infinite variety of diverse foods. Yet all of the thousands of foods available to us in any supermarket today are still made up of only three main nutrients, known as macronutrients: carbohydrates, proteins, and fats. Carbohydrates, proteins, and fats each provide different amounts of energy. One gram of carbohydrate has 3.75 calories of energy, while a gram of protein provides 4 calories of energy. Fat provides the most energy per gram, with 9 calories.

Carbohydrates

Digestion breaks down carbohydrates into sugars, starches (which are sugar molecules bonded together), and fiber. Sugars and starches provide your body with energy. Any energy you do not use gets stored in your body as fat. Fiber is coarse plant matter that cannot be digested. Fresh fruits and vegetables, whole-grain cereals, nuts, peas, and beans are all high in fiber. Even though fiber is not a nutrient, it is very important to your body's health. Fiber, which can only be found in plant foods, aids digestion and can help lower cholesterol. Evidence suggests that a high-fiber diet may lower the risk of some types of cancer. It also helps prevent diseases such as diabetes, heart disease, and an inflammation of the intestine called diverticulitis.

There are two kinds of carbohydrates: simple carbs and complex carbs. Simple carbs are those that are broken down into glucose quickly. Glucose is one of the simplest kinds of sugar molecules and is the body's main source of fuel. The closer something is to glucose, as simple carbs are, the more quickly it is digested and used as fuel. Simple carbs provide an

The grains pictured above—whole wheat bread, white bread, cornmeal, rice, and pasta—are all important sources of carbohydrates.

immediate but short-lived burst of energy. They often leave you feeling less energetic than before eating them. Simple carbs include fruit juice, certain fruits, and highly refined food products like white flour, white rice, sugar, breakfast cereals, white bread, white flour pasta, and candy.

More complex, unrefined, unprocessed carbohydrate foods such as whole fresh fruits, fresh vegetables, brown rice, whole wheat, and bran have more undigestible fiber in them. This means they are broken down into glucose more slowly. Because they release sugar into your bloodstream slowly and steadily, they give you sustained energy over a longer time. In addition, complex carbs usually contain more vitamins and minerals than simple and refined carbs, which are so highly processed that they have lost much of their nutritional value.

Proteins

Proteins are found in every cell of your body. Proteins are made of amino acids, sometimes called the building blocks of life. Your body uses twenty different amino acids. They can be combined, like the ingredients in a recipe, to make the 10,000 or so different proteins of which your body is made. Your body creates eleven of the amino acids it needs to stay in good shape. These are known as the nonessential amino acids. The other—the essential amino acids—must come from the protein in foods. A little protein goes a long way, however: you need only about 1 gram of protein for every kilogram of your body weight (1 kg is about 2.2 pounds). On average, Americans eat about twice that amount.

Proteins come from either animal foods (meat, fish, eggs, and dairy products) or from plant foods (cereals, beans, and nuts). Plant foods do not always have all the essential amino acids your body needs to make the various proteins that build up, maintain, and replace the cell tissues in your body. That is why it is important to eat a variety of vegetables, fruits, and cereals that will provide you with all the amino acids your body needs. Protein from animal sources has a more complete range of amino acid ingredients than do plant foods (with the exception of soy, which contains all of the essential amino acids). But animal protein foods, like meat, fish, and dairy products, have something that most fruits and vegetables do not have much of—fats.

Certain kinds of fish, such as the salmon pictured here, are excellent sources of protein and contain omega-3 fatty acids, which may help fight heart disease.

Fats

Though we tend to think of fats as harmful, they are just as important to the smooth functioning of your body as are carbohydrates and protein. Fats have more than twice as much concentrated energy as either carbohydrates or protein: 9 calories per gram, compared with just 4 calories per gram of protein and 3.75 calories per gram of cabohydrates. In addition, fats help transport and absorb other vitamins in your body.

The amount of fat in your diet is not as important as the type of fat that is found in the foods you eat. Some kinds of fats are better for your health than others. The three main kinds of food fats are saturated fats, unsaturated fats, and trans fats. As we will see below, unsaturated fats are far better for you than either saturated or trans fats.

Saturated fats are mainly animal fats found in meat and dairy products. Some vegetable oils, such as coconut and palm oils, also contain high levels of saturated fats. Unsaturated fats are found mainly in vegetable oils, such as corn, sunflower, soybean, and olive oils. Trans fats are human-made fats. They are produced when hydrogen is pumped through vegetable oil in order to change it from a liquid into a solid. This process, called hydrogenation, turns liquid vegetable oil into a solid fat product such as margarine. Trans fats are listed as hydrogenated or partially hydrogenated vegetable oil on the nutrition labels of packaged foods. The food industry uses cooking oils with a lot of trans fats in them to make cookies, cakes, snack foods, and fast foods.

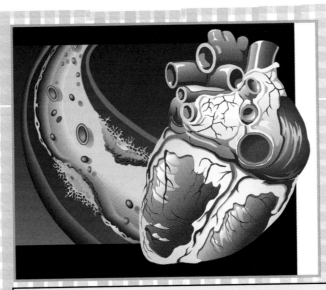

The human heart is seen in the foreground, and in the background is an artery that is clogged with cholesterol and other fatty deposits. The passage through which blood and oxygen flow has become very narrow, restricting the flow of blood and oxygen to the heart, which can lead to coronary heart disease and strokes.

The quality of these different kinds of fats is related to their effect on the cholesterol in your body. Like fats, cholesterol has a bad reputation, though it plays an important role in keeping the body healthy by coating nerve endings and producing hormones. Cholesterol is a substance in body fluids used to keep cell walls healthy and to help build cell tissues. The liver makes cholesterol, which then gets transported in the bloodstream throughout the body by lipoproteins.

Low-density lipoproteins (LDLs) transport cholesterol away from the liver. If there is too much LDL cholesterol in the bloodstream, the cholesterol gets deposited on the walls of your body's arteries. Those cholesterol deposits narrow the arteries, like grease clogging a drain-pipe. Narrowed arteries reduce the flow of blood to your heart. When that happens, your heart does not get enough nutrients and oxygen, which can lead to serious heart disease problems. This is why LDL cho-lesterol is often called "bad" cholesterol.

High-density lipoproteins (HDLs) carry unused cholesterol back from the blood to the liver, which gets rid of it. HDL cholesterol is less likely to be deposited on the walls of arteries. So, HDLs keep your arter-ies clean, thereby reducing the risk of heart disease. This is why HDL cholesterol is often referred to as "good" cholesterol.

What does all this have to do with fats? Unsaturated fats tend to raise the level of good HDL cholesterol and lower the level of bad LDL choles-terol in your blood. Saturated fats tend to raise the level of both types of cholesterol in your blood, both the good HDL and the bad LDL. Trans fats tend to raise the level of bad LDL cholesterol but lower the level of good HDL cholesterol in your blood. So, unsaturated fats actually help to keep your arteries clear. Trans fats and saturated fats can clog up your arteries with cholesterol, which can lead to serious heart disease. That is why unsaturated fats are better for you than saturated fats or trans fats.

Saturated and unsaturated fats are found together in all food fats, but in different proportions. Butter, cheese, and milk, for example, contain

mostly saturated fat. Eggs contain mostly unsaturated fats. Most vegetable oils have a lot of unsaturated fats and less saturated fats.

Vitamins and Minerals

There are two other nutrients in food: vitamins and minerals. These are known as micronutrients. Vitamins are natural substances that are found in both plants and animals. Minerals are substances that originate in rocks and metal ores. Plants obtain minerals from the soil in which they grow, and animals, including humans, absorb these nutrients when they eat plants. Most vitamins and minerals have to come from food because your body can not make them by itself. Unlike fats, protein, and carbohydrates, vitamins and minerals do not provide energy. Instead, they help regulate the body's processes. Compared with the amount of carbohydrates, protein, and fat your body requires, it needs only tiny amounts of each vitamin and mineral to operate properly.

Different vitamins benefit different parts of your body. Without enough of them—or with too much of them sometimes—your body will not work properly. Vitamin C, for example, helps fight infections and keeps your bones, gums, and teeth healthy. Citrus fruits, green peppers, and other fresh fruits and vegetables are the best sources of vitamin C. Vitamin A, also called retinol, plays an important role in vision, bone growth, infection fighting, and regulation of the immune system. Liver, whole milk, eggs, and butter are high in vitamin A. Carrots, cantaloupe, broccoli, and some other fruits and vegetables contain beta-carotene, which the body can convert into vitamin A. Vitamin D helps your body's bones stay strong.

Minerals are inorganic (not living) substances that your body needs to perform many different functions. Calcium, found mostly in your bones and teeth, is the most abundant mineral in your body. Other minerals crucial to our physical health include phosphorus, sodium, potassium, zinc, iron, chlorine, and magnesium. Small amounts of other minerals, such as copper, cobalt, and iodine, are also present in the human body. These trace minerals are found in much smaller amounts, but they, too, are absolutely essential for the body to function properly.

Having lunch at a salad bar is a quick and easy way to eat several servings of fresh vegetables and fruits, while enjoying a low-fat, vitamin- and mineral-packed, and very satisfying meal.

Like vitamins, specific minerals have specific roles to play in the human body. As we have already learned, calcium is the mineral present in our bodies that builds bones and teeth. In order to avoid bone loss or weakening, we need to keep our calcium levels adequate by eating foods rich in calcium, such as milk, cheese, yogurt, spinach, and broccoli. Iron is mainly used by red blood cells to carry oxygen throughout the body as part of the respiratory cycle. An iron deficiency causes a condition called anemia, in which the number of red blood cells decreases and the body gets less oxygen than it needs, resulting in very low energy. Food such as beef, chicken, tuna, egg yolks, green leafy vegetables, and iron-fortified cereals are excellent natural sources of iron.

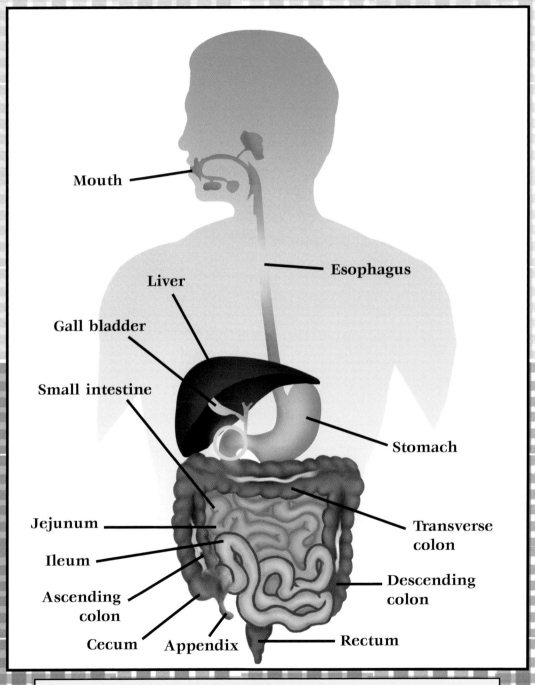

Mouth

Esophagus

Liver

Gall bladder

Small intestine

Stomach

Jejunum

Transverse colon

Ileum

Ascending colon

Descending colon

Cecum

Appendix

Rectum

As this diagram of the digestive system illustrates, the human body is a complex machine. Its many processes are regulated and sustained by the nutrients found in the food we eat.

chapter 2

Digestion and Metabolism

Y our body derives the food energy and nutrients it needs from food by a process called digestion. Nature mixes nutrients and energy to make whole foods, such as fruits, vegetables, and grains. Humans might process these basic foods to create more elaborate products like pasta, bread, soup, vegetable spread, pizza, or cookies. The digestion process uses these nutrients by breaking down the food into its most basic units. This begins happening when you chew food, and it continues in your stomach and intestines. The bloodstream then carries the nutrients to all the cells in your body. Simply put, digestion is the conversion of food into the nutrients and energy that your body needs to stay alive.

Here is how it works. Food goes into your mouth. Your teeth chew the food up into a mush, mixed with saliva. This watery mush is pushed down your esophagus into your stomach. Your stomach walls churn the food up. Acidic stomach juices break the mush into even smaller bits. The food mush then gets pushed out of your stomach into your small intestine.

After reaching the small intestine, the mush is further broken down into carbohydrates, proteins, and fats—the three macronutrients. Each macronutrient is further broken down into its smallest parts. So carbohydrates are converted into sugars, proteins into amino acids, and fats into saturated or unsaturated fatty acids. These tiny particles of sugars, amino acids, and fatty acids now pass through the walls of your small intestine into your bloodstream. The sugars and amino acids are absorbed in your blood. Fats are not absorbed, however. Instead, they remain suspended in your blood in tiny droplets called lipoproteins.

Having reached the bloodstream, the nutrient particles are then carried to every part of your body. Their effect is to provide the body with immediate energy and store leftover energy as fat. Equally important, the nutrients keep your body growing and in a state of good health.

Anything in the food mush that cannot be digested—fiber, undigested bits of food, bacteria—is waste and does not enter your bloodstream from the small intestine. Instead, the waste travels into the large intestine. It stays there as solid feces until it is expelled out of your body through the anus.

Metabolism and the Energy Balance

Food provides the energy your body needs to keep working. Your body burns the energy it gets from the food you eat. You need to eat food regularly to replace the energy the body burns. How much energy you take in from food should be about the same amount of energy your body burns. If you take in more calories than you burn, you will gain weight.

Your metabolism is the rate at which your body burns energy (calories) in order to keep all the cells and functions of your body working properly. Your basal metabolic rate (BMR) is the number of calories your

Working out in a gym or running several miles is not the only way to burn calories, build muscle, and get the heart pumping. Playing games with your friends is a fun and easy way to get exercise and control your weight.

body burns at rest (without doing physical activities). On average, adults need about 1,500 calories a day just to maintain their BMR. How much more energy you burn depends on your age, your weight, what physical activities you do, and whether you are a girl, boy, man, or woman. In order to maintain a healthy weight, the amount of calories you take in through food should be about the same as the amount of calories your body needs for basal metabolism and to perform physical activities. Basal metabolism is the energy required for cell activity, circulation, and breathing by a person at rest. The more physical activities you do, such as exercise or sports, the more food energy (calories) you need to take in.

This is known as the energy balance. The energy you take in (as food) should balance the energy being spent on basal metabolism and physical activities. If you eat 2,500 calories of food a day, your body should burn about 2,500 calories a day. If you eat a lot and take in more calories than you burn, the unused energy will be stored in the body as fat. You will gain weight. If you take in fewer calories than you burn, your body will take the extra energy it needs from the fat you have stored in your body. As your body burns up more of this stored fat, you will lose weight.

This simple formula expresses the relationship between calories, metabolism, and weight change:

Calories in (what you eat) balanced against calories out (what your body burns) = Weight change

Even if you exercise regularly and are very active, you still have to watch what you eat and be aware of how many calories you are taking in. Refuel your body every day with lots of low-fat, low-calorie fruits and vegetables.

If you take in 2,500 calories a day and burn only 2,000 calories a day, you are eating more than your body is burning, and you will gain weight. If you take in 2,000 calories a day and burn 2,500 calories a day, your body is burning more energy than is provided by the food you are eating, and you will lose weight. If you take in about 2,000 calories a day and burn about 2,000 calories in a day, you are eating just enough food to meet your body's energy needs, and your weight will stay about the same.

It is almost impossible to achieve an exact balance between the calories you take in and those you burn on any given day. By keeping this formula in mind, however, you can come close to the proper energy balance and maintain a steady healthy weight over time. To check on how well you are achieving a good energy balance and controlling your weight, you can use a formula called the body mass index.

The Body Mass Index

The body mass index (BMI) is a formula used to find out if you are underweight, overweight, or about the right weight. A BMI in the range of nineteen to twenty-five is considered a healthy weight. Anything under nineteen is considered underweight, while a reading over twenty-five indicates that a person is overweight. A BMI of thirty or more indicates obesity, a condition that is characterized by excessive body fat.

To determine your body mass index, use the following formula:

1. Divide your weight in pounds by your height in inches.
2. Divide that answer by your height in inches.
3. Multiply that answer by 703.

Let's take, for example, a person who weighs 150 pounds and is 5 feet 6 inches (or 66 inches) tall.

1. Divide weight in pounds (150) by height in inches (66) = 2.27
2. Divide that answer (2.27) by height in inches (66) = 0.034
3. Multiply that answer (0.034) by 703 = 24.2

This person's BMI—twenty-four—is within the normal range of nineteen to twenty-five, so he or she is at a healthy weight. Now use your own

While it is a good idea to watch your calorie intake and exercise regularly, try to avoid getting too preoccupied with your weight. With the help of your doctor, get an idea of what a healthy weight for your body type is and try to stay within that range without weighing yourself constantly or obsessing about pounds lost or gained.

weight and height to calculate your BMI. Follow steps one through three as shown in the previous example.

Your Daily Calorie Requirements

Want a simple, approximate way to find out how many calories a day you need? Multiply your weight in kilograms by twenty-nine if you are not very active or by thirty-three if you are very active. If you are moderately active, choose a number somewhere in between the two extremes. To convert pounds to kilograms, multiply your weight in pounds by 0.454.

Let's say you weigh 110 pounds. That is 50 kilograms (110 × .454 = 50). Let's say you are moderately active, so we will multiply 50 × 31. That is 1,550; so your body needs about 1,550 calories a day to fuel its processes and provide you with the energy you need for your moderate activity. If you are 110 pounds and very active, multiply 50 by 33. You will need 1,650 calories a day.

chapter 3

The Food Guide Pyramid

The food guide pyramid is a graphic nutritional guide developed by the U.S. Department of Agriculture (USDA) and supported by the Department of Health and Human Services (HHS). The pyramid is based on the USDA's research on what foods Americans eat and what nutrients are in these foods. Based on these findings, the food pyramid tries to guide Americans in how to make the best choices to create a healthy and nutritious diet. The pyramid and a related USDA booklet, "The Food Guide Pyramid" (http://www.pueblo.gsa.gov/cic_text/food/food-pyramid/main.htm), will help you choose what and how much to eat from each food group to obtain the proper balance of nutrients you need without taking in too many calories, fat, cholesterol, sugar, or sodium.

The pyramid has been attacked by critics who say some parts of it are vague, inaccurate, or misleading. Yet when it is used in conjunction with the USDA's food pyramid pamphlet, a clear and detailed series of recommendations are presented. It is important to read both the pamphlet and the criticisms of it to learn more about good nutrition and help you adopt a balanced and healthy diet that works for you.

The Food Pyramid

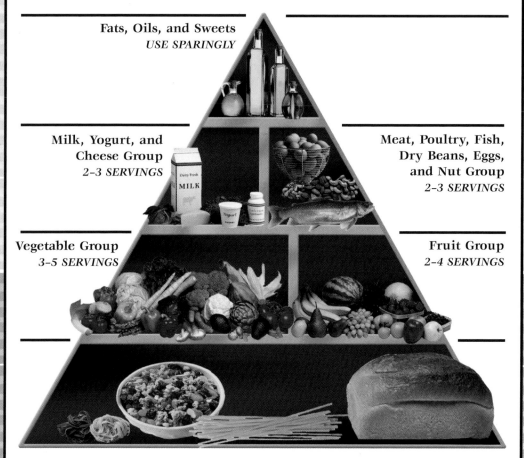

Fats, Oils, and Sweets
USE SPARINGLY

Milk, Yogurt, and
Cheese Group
2–3 SERVINGS

Meat, Poultry, Fish,
Dry Beans, Eggs,
and Nut Group
2–3 SERVINGS

Vegetable Group
3–5 SERVINGS

Fruit Group
2–4 SERVINGS

Bread, Cereal, Rice, and Pasta Group
6–11 SERVINGS

This version of the USDA's food pyramid shows what kinds of healthy foods can be found in each of the pyramid's six categories: grains; vegetables; fruits; dairy; protein; and fats, oils, and sugars. The size of the compartment containing each type of food indicates the relative proportion of your diet it should represent. Grains, vegetables, and fruits should make up the bulk of your diet, while servings of dairy and protein should be fewer. Oil, sweets, and fats should be eaten sparingly.

The Food Pyramid's Message

Throughout the 1980s and 1990s, the USDA published guides about healthy eating and nutrition, including an annual healthy eating guide, "A Pattern for Daily Food Choices." Based on rising obesity rates, however, it seemed that Americans were still not getting the USDA's message about eating a variety of foods in a nutritious balance and in moderate amounts. To help simplify its message and present its dietary recommendations in a clear, easy-to-read format, the USDA needed to design a simple graphic image that would quickly convey the basics of good nutrition. The result was the food guide pyramid, which was first introduced to Americans in 1992.

The basic message of the food pyramid and the USDA guidelines that accompany it is to eat well and be active in order to live longer. Its general recommendations are:

○ Eat a variety of foods to get the energy, protein, vitamins, minerals, and fiber you need for good health.

○ Balance the food you eat with physical activity. Maintain or improve your weight to reduce your chances of having high blood pressure, heart disease, a stroke, certain cancers, and the most common kind of diabetes.

○ Choose a diet with plenty of grain products, vegetables, and fruits, which provide needed vitamins, minerals, fiber, and complex carbohydrates, and can help you lower your intake of fat.

○ Choose a diet low in fat and cholesterol to reduce your risk of heart attack and certain types of cancer and to help you maintain a healthy weight.

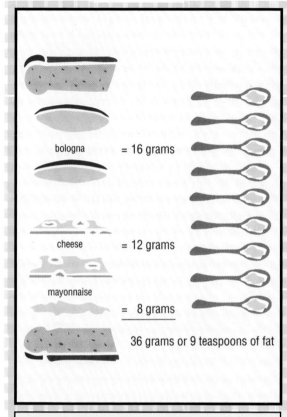

bologna   = 16 grams

cheese   = 12 grams

mayonnaise
              = 8 grams

36 grams or 9 teaspoons of fat

This USDA diagram provides a breakdown of the fat content of a typical bologna and cheese sandwich.

○ Choose a diet moderate in sugars. A diet with lots of sugars has too many calories and too few nutrients for most people and can contribute to tooth decay.

○ Choose a diet moderate in salt to help reduce your risk of high blood pressure.

The Pyramid's Structure and Recommendations

The food guide pyramid shows the recommended number of servings of grains, fruits, vegetables, dairy foods, proteins, fats, and sugars you should eat per day. The broad base of the pyramid is filled with foods you need more of in any given day. The narrow tip is devoted to foods and nutrients that should be eaten more sparingly. The food pyramid includes six food groups and the following recommended daily servings from each:

1. Grains: bread, cereals, rice, and pasta (six to eleven servings)
2. Vegetables (three to five servings)

3.   Fruits (two to four servings)
4.   Meat (protein): beef, poultry, fish, eggs, beans, and nuts (two to three servings)
5.   Dairy: milk, yogurt, and cheese (two to three servings)
6.   Fats, oils, and sweets (sparingly)

Grains

At the base of the pyramid is the grain group. The USDA recommends that you eat from six to eleven servings of grains each day—more than any other type of food. This group includes bread, rice, pasta, and cereal. Choose whole grains such as whole wheat bread, brown rices, and whole wheat pasta. All of these foods are excellent sources of carbohydrates.

Vegetables

The next level on the pyramid is the vegetable group. The USDA recommends that you eat between three and five servings of vegetables each day. Vegetables provide a variety of vitamins and minerals. For example, dark-green vegetables, such as broccoli and spinach, provide vitamin A, vitamin C, iron, and more. It is a good idea to try to eat many different kinds of vegetables so that you get the widest possible variety of vitamins and minerals.

Fruits

Fruits are the next group represented on the pyramid, alongside vegetables. The food pyramid suggests that you eat two to four servings of fruit each day. Most fruits are a good source of vitamins A and C, as well as fiber

The food pyramid recommends that you eat three to five servings of vegetables a day. As these market stalls overflowing with artichokes, celery, potatoes, tomatoes, peas, and peppers indicate, vegetable options are as varied as they are delicious.

and potassium. As with vegetables, it is best if you eat a variety of fruits in order to benefit from a wide range of vitamins. Canned fruits and fruit juices are not as nutritious as fresh fruit, mainly because they often contain added sugar.

Protein

The next level of the pyramid is occupied by protein. Meat, poultry, fish, beans, eggs, and nuts all fall into this category. Only two to three servings of protein per day are recommended. The average individual needs to consume about eight grams of protein per twenty pounds of body weight daily. Since that is a relatively small amount, few Americans, not even vegetarians, are likely to suffer from a protein deficiency.

Dairy

Dairy is the next food group to appear in the pyramid. Dairy foods such as milk, yogurt, and cheese provide your body with calcium, important for the development and strengthening of bones. The USDA recommends that children and teenagers have three to four servings of dairy each day to help their growing bodies get the calcium they need. Calcium remains important beyond childhood and adolescence, however. Up until about

Iron is important for healthy blood and many chemical reactions in your body. Calcium helps strengthen bones. Both minerals are found in many foods, especially milk, cheese, green leafy vegetables, fish, meat, and poultry.

age thirty, the body stores calcium for the future. As we get older, we begin to lose bone density. As a result, our bones become more brittle and breakable. Stored calcium slows this bone loss and helps keep bones as strong as possible for as long as possible.

Fats, Oils, and Sugars

Sitting at the very top of the pyramid is the fats, oils, and sugars section. These types of foods include candy, baked goods, sodas, salad dressings, and spreads (such as mayonnaise). Most of these foods have little nutritional value and a lot of fat or calories. The USDA recommends that you eat the least amount of these foods.

chapter 4

Possible Improvements to the Food Pyramid

Not everyone agrees with the composition of the food guide pyramid. Critics have pointed out a number of ways it could be improved.

Fats

Critics say the food pyramid groups all fats and oils together without distinguishing between good and bad fats. They say it ignores the health benefits of unsaturated fats, which might prevent heart diseases. They suggest revisions to the pyramid that will encourage Americans to eat more foods containing unsaturated fats (such as vegetable oils, fish, and nuts) and less food with saturated fats (such as red meat, whole milk, and eggs) and trans fats (found in margarine, fried foods, crackers, candies, baked goods, cookies, snack foods, salad dressings, and many processed foods).

Carbohydrates

The food guide pyramid groups together all kinds of carbo-hydrate foods—bread, pasta, rice, cereals—without saying which ones are healthier. Whole-grain foods (such as whole-meal bread and brown rice) are more nutritious and have more fiber than refined grain foods (such as white bread, white rice, and pasta). Refined grains have had their nutritious bran and germ layers removed by the milling process. Critics say the pyramid should show that eating whole-grain foods is healthier than eating refined grain foods.

Potatoes

Some critics point out that the food pyramid groups all fruits and vegetables together, including potatoes. Although potatoes are rich in potassium, vitamin C, and fiber, the carbohydrates in potatoes are simple rather than

The carbohydrates present in the natural sugars of fruits, such as apples, are complex, unlike the simple carbs of white flour, refined sugar, and candy. Complex carbs release energy more slowly and steadily and contain more vitamins and minerals than do simple carbs.

complex. They release their sugars quickly into the bloodstream, creating a sudden surge of energy that is soon burned off. Americans eat about 90 pounds (40 kg) of processed potatoes per person per year. A lot of that is in the form of fast-food french fries, which, because they are fried, are loaded with trans fats. They are much higher in fat calories than even

Potatoes are rich in potassium, vitamin C, fiber, and cancer-fighting antioxidants. When fried, however, they lose much of their nutritional value and can become an unhealthy food. An average eight-ounce serving of french fries contains roughly 480 calories and at least 13 grams of fat. An eight-ounce baked or boiled potato contains only 160 calories and 0 grams of fat.

hamburgers. For this reason, some critics say that potatoes should be separated from the vegetable category on the food pyramid. Instead, they believe that potatoes should be placed toward the tip of the pyramid, with the sweets, oils, and fats, to indicate that they should be eaten sparingly.

Proteins

The food pyramid groups together all high-protein foods such as meat, fish, nuts, beans, and eggs. However, as critics point out, some of these sources of protein are healthier than others. For example, certain cuts of red meat can contain a lot of saturated fat. A diet high in meat products has also been linked with some kinds of cancer. Processed meat products like sausages, bacon, salami, and bologna are often loaded with salt and preservatives and are high in saturated fats. Nuts, beans, and fish are all excellent sources of protein that are low in saturated fat. Nuts and beans have the added advantage of also being high in fiber. Some nutritionists believe that these healthy proteins should be placed lower on the food pyramid, with more recommended servings a day. Beef and processed meats should be moved higher up the pyramid, with fewer recommended servings.

Dairy

Some nutritionists believe that the calcium recommendations of the food pyramid encourage too much consumption of dairy foods. Although milk, cheese, and other dairy foods are a convenient way to get calcium into your diet, they are also often high in saturated fats (you should choose low- or non-fat dairy products, which have actually been linked with fat loss). These critics also question whether people need to eat as much calcium-rich foods as the pyramid recommends. They argue that low-fat leafy green vegetables, such as spinach, are better sources of calcium than most fat-rich

In order to achieve the best results, exercise and good nutrition must go hand in hand. Neither alone can provide you with maximum physical and mental health.

dairy foods. For this reason, critics say the food pyramid should show fewer serving of dairy foods.

Calories and Physical Activity

The food pyramid graphic says nothing about the importance of physical activity to a healthier life (although the text of the accompanying pamphlet does). The pyramid does not show the connection between exercise, calorie burning, energy balance, and weight control. This crucial health information, critics say, should appear right at the base of the pyramid, to emphasize its importance.

Conclusion

According to the Harvard School of Public Health, excess weight leads to at least 300,000 deaths per year in the United States and costs more than $70 billion each year in medical costs. Obesity now accounts for more deaths; serious, long-lasting illness; and poor quality of life than either smoking or alcohol dependency.

Maintaining a healthy weight is as important as achieving a healthy balance of nutrients in your diet. Being overweight or obese puts more strain on the body, particularly the heart, which has to work much harder to pump blood throughout an overweight body. Some of the other health risks associated with being overweight or obese include early death, some cancers, infertility (the inability to conceive and bear children), heart disease, and diabetes (a disorder in which the blood contains excessive amounts of sugar).

More and more Americans are becoming overweight or obese. According to the National Heart, Lung, and Blood Institute and the Centers for Disease Control, about 35 percent of Americans are considered overweight

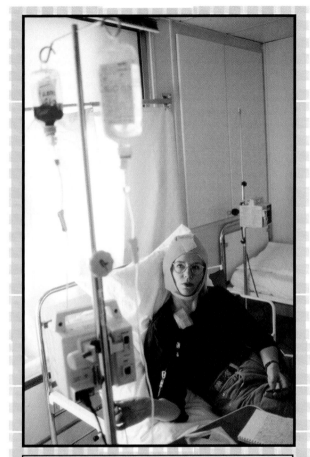

This woman is receiving chemotherapy to treat her breast cancer. A diet that is low in fat, low in calories, and rich in vitamins and minerals may help prevent various cancers and other serious diseases.

(but not obese). This figure has not changed much since 1980, when 33 percent of Americans were overweight. However, the number of Americans who are obese has almost doubled since 1980, from about 15 percent of the population then to almost 30 percent now. Almost 15 percent of American children and adolescents are now overweight or obese, twice the childhood obesity rate of the 1970s. All told, more than 100 million Americans are now overweight or obese.

If you care about your health, about being underweight or overweight, about getting a serious disease, or about dying too young, then you must also care about what you eat. Learning about nutrition is the first step in creating a better diet and a healthier lifestyle.

The next step is putting that knowledge into practice. Think about what you eat—about the calories you consume; the energy you burn through exercise; and the amount, variety, and nutritional value of the food in your daily diet. Use the food pyramid as a guide to choosing the widest variety and most nutritious of foods and as a tool in achieving a healthy balance among the six main food groups.

Getting into the habit of thinking about nutrition in this way will encourage a healthy lifestyle built upon a nutritious diet and physical activity.

The first step is beginning to care about what you eat.

Once nutritious and delicious meals and snacks become a daily habit, you will probably not find junk food and fast food very tempting anymore.

Caring about what you eat is caring about yourself. After all, you are what you eat.

Glossary

calorie A unit of measure that indicates how much energy a food will provide.

carbohydrate An essential structural part of living cells and a macronutrient that provides the human body with the energy it needs to function. Carbohydrates are found in grains, starches, fruits, and sugar.

cholesterol A substance found in animal tissues and some foods (such as red meat and eggs) that is used in building cell tissues and hormones. In humans, it can build up in the arteries, causing dangerous blockages.

coronary heart disease A condition in which blood flow to the heart is restricted by cholesterol buildup in the arteries.

fiber Coarse, indigestible plant matter that aids digestion and can help lower cholesterol.

high-density lipoprotein (HDL) A substance that transports cholesterol easily through the bloodstream and is associated with a decreased risk of coronary heart disease; often called "good" cholesterol.

low-density lipoprotein (LDL) A substance that transports cholesterol and is associated with a greater risk of coronary heart disease; often referred to as "bad" cholesterol.

minerals Inorganic substances found in nature and vital to the nutrition of plants, animals, and humans.

nutrition The processes by which an individual takes in and utilizes food material.

obese Excessively overweight; generally at least 20 percent more than one's ideal body weight.

protein A macronutrient found in meats, beans, nuts, and some other foods that is responsible for repairing and building cells in the body.

saturated fat A fat or fatty acid that has been linked to increased risk of coronary heart disease and is solid at room temperature.

trans fat An unhealthy substance that is made when food manufacturers turn liquid oils into solid fats by adding hydrogen (in a process called hydrogenation). Trans fat can be found in vegetable shortenings, some margarines, crackers, cookies, snack foods, and other foods made with or fried in partially hydrogenated oils.

unsaturated fat An oil or fatty acid that may reduce levels of LDL cholesterol.

vitamin Any of a group of organic substances essential to the nutrition of most animals and some plants. Vitamins are present in food and are sometimes produced in the body, but they do not provide energy.

For More Information

The American Dietetic Association
120 South Riverside Plaza, Suite 2000
Chicago, IL 60606-6995
(800) 877-1600
Web site: http://www.eatright.org

American Public Health Association
800 I Street NW
Washington, DC 20001
(202) 777-2742
Web site: http://www.apha.org

Food and Nutrition Information Center
Agricultural Research Service, USDA
National Agricultural Library, Room 105
10301 Baltimore Avenue
Beltsville, MD 20705-2351
(301) 504-5719
Web site: http://www.nal.usda.gov/fnic

National Institutes of Health (NIH)
9000 Rockville Pike
Bethesda, MD 20892
(301) 496-4000
Web site: http://www.nih.gov

U.S. Department of Agriculture (USDA)
Food and Nutrition Service
3101 Park Center Drive, Room 926
Alexandria, VA 22302
Web site: http://www.fns.usda.gov/fns/default.htm

U.S. Food and Drug Administration (FDA)
Center for Food Safety and Applied Nutrition
5600 Fishers Lane
Rockville, MD 20857
(888) INFO-FDA
Web site: http://vm.cfsan.fda.gov/list.html

Web Sites

Due to the changing nature of Internet links, the Rosen Publishing Group, Inc., has developed an online list of Web sites related to the subject of this book. This site is updated regularly. Please use this link to access the list:

http://www.rosenlinks.com/linu/fpbn

For Further Reading

Frost, Helen, and Gail Saunders-Smith, Ph.D. *The Food Guide Pyramid.* Mankato, MN: Capstone Press, 2000.

Kaehler, Kathy, and Connie Church. *Teenage Fitness: Get Fit, Look Good, and Feel Great!* New York: Harper-Resource, 2001.

Kalbacken, Joan. *The Food Pyramid.* New York: Children's Press, 1998.

Leedy, Loreen. *The Edible Pyramid: Good Eating Every Day.* New York: Holiday House, 1996.

Rockwell, Lizzy. *Good Enough to Eat: A Kid's Guide to Food and Nutrition.* New York: HarperCollins Publishers, 1999.

Rondeau, Amanda, and Monica Marx. *The Food Pyramid.* South Pasadena, CA: Sandcastle Publishing, 2002.

Salter, Charles A. *The Nutrition-Fitness Link: How Diet Can Help Your Body and Mind.* Brookfield, CT: Millbrook Press, 1993.

VanCleave, Janice. *Janice VanCleave's Food and Nutrition for Every Kid: Easy Activities That Make Learning Science Fun.* New York: Wiley, 1999.

Walker, Pam, and Elaine Wood. *The Digestive System.* San Diego: Greenhaven Press, 2002.

Bibliography

"America's Eating Habits: Changes and Consequences." USDA.gov, 2000. Retrieved June 2004 (http://www.ers.usda.gov/publications/aib750/aib750.pdf).

Bender, Arnold E., and David A. Bender. *Oxford Dictionary of Food & Nutrition.* Oxford, England: Oxford University Press, 1995.

British Nutrition Foundation. *Nutrition Facts.* London: British Nutrition Foundation, 2004.

Cameron, Allan G., and Brian A. Fox. *Food Science, Nutrition, and Health.* London: Arnold/Hodder Headline, 1997.

Clark, Linda. *Know Your Nutrition.* New Canaan, CT: Keats Publishing, 1981.

Davis, Adelle. *Let's Stay Healthy: A Guide to Lifelong Nutrition.* New York: Harcourt, 1981.

Food Standards Agency. *Manual of Nutrition.* Norwich, England: The Stationery Office, 2002.

"The Nutrition Source: Knowledge for Healthy Eating." Harvard School of Public Health, 2004. Retrieved June 2004 (http://www.hsph.harvard.edu/nutritionsource/).

Schlosser, Eric. *Fast Food Nation: The Dark Side of the All-American Meal.* New York: HarperPerennial, 2002.

Sharon, Dr. Michael. *Complete Nutrition: How to Live in Total Health.* London: Prion Books, 2002.

Shell, Ellen Ruppel. *The Hungry Gene: The Inside Story of the Obesity Industry.* New York: Grove Press, 2003.

Stanford, Dell, ed. *The Fat, Fibre, and Carbohydrate Counter*. London: Murdoch Books, 2001.

United States Department of Agriculture. "Nutrition and Your Health: Dietary Guidelines for Americans." USDA.gov, 2000. Retrieved June 2004 (http://www.usda.gov/cnpp/DietGd.pdf).

Willett, Walter C., M.D. *Eat, Drink, and Be Healthy*. New York: Free Press/Simon & Schuster, 2003.

Willett, Walter C., M.D., and Meir J. Stampfer. "Rebuilding the Food Pyramid." Scientific American Online, January 2003. Retrieved June 2004 (http://www.sciam.com/article.cfm?chanID = sa006&colID = 1&articleID = 0007C5B6-7152-1DF6-9733809EC588EEDF).

World Cancer Research Fund. *Food, Nutrition, and Cancer*. Washington, DC: American Institute for Cancer Research, 1997.

Index

About the Author

Graham Faiella writes mainly nonfiction books on subjects related to the sea or anything else that interests him. He is originally from Bermuda and has lived in the United Kingdom since 1974.

Photo Credits

Cover (background images), back cover images, title page (background images), pp. 3, 4, 7, 19, 25, 32, 37, 40, 42, 44, 45, 47 © David Wasserman/Artville; cover image, title page image © Stockfood; p. 5 © AP/Wide World Photos; pp. 6, 22 © Bill Lai/Index Stock Imagery; p. 8 © Tim Boyle/Getty Images; p. 11 photo by Scott Bauer/Agricultural Research Service/United States Department of Agriculture; p. 13 © Blair Howard/Index Stock Imagery; p. 14 © Images.com/Corbis; p. 17 © Bob Rowan/Progessive Image/Corbis; p. 18 Tahara Anderson; p. 21 © Rob Morsch/Corbis; p. 24 © Richard Hutchings/Corbis; p. 26 © Photodisc/2004 Punchstock except image of fish © Image Club; p. 28 courtesy of the Center for Nutrition Policy and Promotion/United States Department of Agriculture; pp. 30, 38 © Owen Franken/Corbis; p. 31 © Photodisc Green/Getty Images; p. 33 © Craig Witkowski/Index Stock Imagery; p. 34 © Gary Houlder/Corbis; p. 36 © E. H. Wallop/Corbis; p. 39 © Tomas del Amo/Index Stock Imagery.

Designer: Geri Fletcher; **Editor:** John Kemmerer